Horace Satire 1.9
THE BOOR

TEACHER'S GUIDE

For College and Advanced Placement Preparation

Margaret A. Brucia
Madeleine M. Henry

Bolchazy-Carducci Publishers, Inc.
Wauconda, Illinois

Editor
Laurie K. Haight

Contributing Editor
Gaby Huebner

Cover Design & Typography
Charlene M. Hernandez

Cover Illustration
Fragment of man (poet?) reading
From a photograph taken by M. A. Brucia

The Latin text of *Satire* 1.9 is reprinted from
Horace: Opera, ed. Edward C. Wickham and H. W. Garrod
(Oxford: Clarendon Press, 1963)
by permission of Oxford University Press

© Copyright 1998 Bolchazy-Carducci Publishers, Inc.

Bolchazy-Carducci Publishers, Inc.
1000 Brown Street, Unit 101
Wauconda, Illinois 60084 USA
http://www.bolchazy.com

Printed in the United States of America
1998
by Publisher's Graphics

ISBN 0-86516-429-0

Contents

Preface v

Horace *Satire* 1.9: The Boor 3

Horace *Satire* 1.9: Literal Translation 9

Questions for discussion 13

Preface

We have written the translation and questions for discussion as an aid for teachers. The translation aims to be literal rather than literary and as readable as one can make such an animal. The questions for discussion will, we hope, open doors to further exploration and greater appreciation; they are neither prescriptive nor indicative of the direction that Advanced Placement test questions may take.

The large-print reproduction of the text is meant as an aid to teachers in preparing exams, quizzes, or materials for overhead projection.

Horace Satire 1.9
THE BOOR

Satire 1.9

Ibam forte Via Sacra, sicut meus est mos,

nescio quid meditans nugarum, totus in illis.

Accurrit quidam notus mihi nomine tantum,

arreptaque manu "Quid agis, dulcissime rerum?"

"Suaviter, ut nunc est," inquam, "et cupio omnia quae vis." 5

Cum adsectaretur, "Num quid vis?" occupo. At ille

"Noris nos" inquit; "docti sumus." Hic ego "Pluris

hoc" inquam "mihi eris." Misere discedere quaerens,

ire modo ocius, interdum consistere, in aurem

dicere nescio quid puero, cum sudor ad imos 10

manaret talos. "O te, Bolane, cerebri

felicem!" aiebam tacitus, cum quidlibet ille

garriret, vicos, urbem laudaret. Ut illi

nil respondebam, "Misere cupis" inquit "abire;

iamdudum video: sed nil agis; usque tenebo;   15

persequar hinc quo nunc iter est tibi." "Nil opus est te

circumagi: quendam volo visere non tibi notum:

trans Tiberim longe cubat is, prope Caesaris hortos."

"Nil habeo quod agam et non sum piger: usque sequar te."

Demitto auriculas, ut iniquae mentis asellus,   20

cum gravius dorso subiit onus. Incipit ille:

"Si bene me novi non Viscum pluris amicum,

non Varium facies: nam quis me scribere plures

aut citius possit versus? Quis membra movere

mollius? Invideat quod et Hermogenes ego canto."   25

Interpellandi locus hic erat: "Est tibi mater,

cognati, quis te salvo est opus?" "Haud mihi quisquam:

omnes composui." "Felices! Nunc ego resto.

Confice; namque instat fatum mihi triste, Sabella

quod puero cecinit divina mota anus urna: 30

Hunc neque dira venena nec hosticus auferet ensis,

nec laterum dolor aut tussis, nec tarda podagra;

garrulus hunc quando consumet cumque: loquaces,

si sapiat, vitet, simul atque adoleverit aetas."

Ventum erat ad Vestae, quarta iam parte diei 35

praeterita, et casu tunc respondere vadato

debebat; quod ni fecisset, perdere litem.

"Si me amas" inquit "paulum hic ades." "Interam si

aut valeo stare aut novi civilia iura;

et propero quo scis." "Dubius sum quid faciam" inquit, 40

"tene relinquam an rem." "Me, sodes." "Non faciam" ille,

et praecedere coepit. Ego, ut contendere durum est

cum victore, sequor. "Maecenas quomodo tecum?"

6 • Horace Satire 1.9: The Boor

hinc repetit: "Paucorum hominum et mentis bene sanae;

nemo dexterius fortuna est usus. Haberes   45

magnum adiutorem, posset qui ferre secundas,

hunc hominem velles si tradere: dispeream ni

summosses omnes." "Non isto vivimus illic

quo tu rere modo; domus hac nec purior ulla est

nec magis his aliena malis; nil mi officit" inquam   50

"ditior hic aut est quia doctior; est locus uni

cuique suus." "Magnum narras, vix credibile." "Atqui

sic habet." "Accendis, quare cupiam magis illi

proximus esse." "Velis tantummodo, quae tua virtus,

expugnabis; et est qui vinci possit, eoque   55

difficiles aditus primos habet." "Haud mihi deero:

muneribus servos corrumpam; non, hodie si

exclusus fuero, desistam; tempora quaeram;

occurram in triviis; deducam. Nil sine magno

vita labore dedit mortalibus." Haec dum agit, ecce 60

Fuscus Aristius occurrit, mihi carus et illum

qui pulchre nosset. Consistimus. "Unde venis?" et

"Quo tendis?" rogat et respondet. Vellere coepi,

et prensare manu lentissima bracchia, nutans,

distorquens oculos, ut me eriperet. Male salsus 65

ridens dissimulare: meum iecur urere bilis.

"Certe nescio quid secreto velle loqui te

aiebas mecum." "Memini bene, sed meliore

tempore dicam: hodie tricesima sabbata: vin tu

curtis Iudaeis oppedere?" "Nulla mihi" inquam 70

"religio est." "At mi: sum paulo infirmior, unus

multorum: ignosces: alias loquar." Huncine solem

tam nigrum surrexe mihi! Fugit improbus ac me

sub cultro linquit. Casu venit obvius illi

adversarius et "Quo tu turpissime?" magna 75

inclamat voce, et "Licet antestari?" Ego vero

oppono auriculam. Rapit in ius: clamor utrimque:

undique concursus. Sic me servavit Apollo.

Literal Translation

I happened to be walking on the Via Sacra, as is my custom, thinking about some trifles, entirely absorbed in them. A certain person, known to me only by name, runs up to me and, after my hand is grabbed, says, "What are you up to, my dearest pal?"

"Just fine at the moment," I say, "and I trust all things are as you wish them to be." When he keeps following, I seize an opportunity—"You don't want anything, do you?" But he says, "[I want that] you get to know me, I'm educated!"

At this point, I say, "You'll be of greater value to me because of this." Trying desperately to leave, now and again I went faster, meanwhile I stopped, I said something or another into my slave's ear while the sweat kept running down to the bottom of my ankles.

I started to say quietly to myself, "O Bolanus, you are fortunate to be hotheaded," when that fellow began to babble about anything and everything, chattering about the neighborhoods, praising the city. When I continued not to respond to him, he said,

"You desperately want to leave; I've been noticing now for a long time: but you're doing nothing [about it]. I'll stick with you to the end; I'll trail you from here to wher[ever] your route takes you now."

"There's no need for you to be dragged around: I want to visit a certain person you don't know. He's sick in bed all the way across the Tiber, near the gardens of Caesar."

"I've got nothing to do and I'm no slug; I'll follow you to the end!"

I droop my ears like a little donkey with a bad attitude, when it takes a rather heavy load on its back. He begins:

"If I know myself well, you wouldn't consider Viscus or Varius a more valuable friend. For who can write more verses, and more quickly, than I can? Who moves his limbs more gracefully? And Hermogenes might envy what I sing."

Here was the place to interrupt! "You do have a mother, relatives, who need you safe and sound?"

"I have hardly anybody: I've buried them all."

"The lucky ones! Now I'm left. Finish me off, for the sad fate is upon me that the aged Sabellian hag prophesied for me, when I was a lad, after her divine urn had been shaken: *Neither dreadful poison, nor enemy sword will carry off this one, nor a pain in the sides, nor a cough, nor limping gout. A talkaholic will some day waste this boy away. If he is wise, let him avoid the prolix and he will live to grow up.*"

We had come to the shrine of Vesta, a quarter of the day now having slipped past. At that time, it so happened that he had to appear in court, a bond having been posted. If he didn't do this, he would lose his case.

"Please," he says, "come [to court] here for a little while."

"Damn me if I have the financial means to stand up for you or if I know about civil law; besides, you know where I'm hurrying."

"I don't know what to do," he says, "whether to abandon you or my case."

"Me, please!"

"I won't do it," he says, and he begins to go ahead.

Because it's hard to fight with a winner, I follow.

"How is Maecenas with you?" He says. Then he repeats: "[I hear] he has few friends and much sense. Nobody has used good fortune so skillfully. You'd have a great helper who could bring about favorable situations, if you'd only care to introduce yours truly. I'll be damned if you wouldn't remove all the obstacles!"

"We don't operate the way you think there. No home is simpler than this one and more alien to these evils. It makes no difference to me," I say, "that somebody is rather wealthy, or is better educated. Each one has his own spot."

"You're telling a tall tale—that's hardly believable."

"But that's how it is."

"You're getting me excited; that's why I want even more to be close to him."

"Just you wish it, that's your strong suit, you'll conquer. He's the sort who can be won over—that's why he has difficult first approaches."

"I'll leave no stone unturned: I'll bribe his slaves with gifts! I won't stop if I'm shut out today. I'll look for opportunities, I'll accost him at the crossroads, I'll escort him! Life has given mortals nothing without great effort."

While he is carrying on like this, lo and behold, Aristius Fuscus enters, a dear friend and someone who knows that man well. We stop.

"From where are you coming?" And "To where are you headed?" he asks and answers.

I began to pluck and press the softest parts of his arms with my hand, nodding, rolling my eyes, so he'd rescue me. Inappropriately witty, laughing, he pretends [not to understand]! Bile burns my liver.

"Of course, you were saying you wanted to talk over something with me in private" [I attempted].

"I remember quite well, but I'll tell you at a better time. Today is the thirtieth Sabbath. You don't want to annoy the circumcized Jews, do you?"

"Religion is not important to me," I say.

"But [it is] to me; I am a little more susceptible, one of the many. You'll pardon [me]; I'll speak [with you] somewhere else."

Such a dark day dawned for me then! The scoundrel flees and leaves me under the knife.

By chance, the plaintiff comes up to that man and shouts in a loud voice, "Where are you going, you loser?" And [to me], "will you witness this?"

Indeed, I offer my ear [to be touched as a sign of assent]. He takes [us] under jurisdiction—noise on either side—from all sides a tumult.

Thus Apollo saved me!

Questions for Discussion

1. In lines 1–21 (*Ibam forte...subiit onus*), the narrator establishes a distinct contrast between his own mood and personality and that of the individual who joins him. Referring to the Latin, describe how Horace creates this contrast.

2. What adjectives might you use to describe the narrator's personality as he presents himself in lines 1–5? Use both English adjectives and Latin adjectives not found in the passage.

3. What metaphor does Horace suggest with his use of the word *occupo* (line 6)?

4. What is the effect of the Boor's use of the plural in line 7?

5. Explain the sarcasm in the words *pluris...eris* (lines 7–8).

6. Why do the words *Misere...laudaret* (lines 8–13) cause us to smile?

7. Find the words that create a sharp contrast between the poet and the Boor in lines 12–14.

8. In an effort to rid himself of the Boor's company, the poet mentions three things about the person he is purportedly setting out to visit that he hopes will dissuade the Boor from following him (lines 17–18). What are they? Quote the appropriate Latin phrases.

9. In the simile introduced with the word *ut* (line 20), to whom and to what are *asellus* and *onus* compared?

10. Explain the effect of the alliterative *m* in the sentence *Quis membra movere mollius* (lines 24–25).

11. Explain the sarcasm in the outburst *Felices!* (line 28).

12. What is the significance of the words of the prophetess *atque adoleverit aetas* (line 34)?

13. Explain the Boor's dilemma as seen in lines 40–41.

14 • Horace Satire 1.9: The Boor

14. Give two qualities of Maecenas as he is described in lines 44–45.

15. How does the Boor's description of his plan to gain access to Maecenas in lines 56–60 make the poet's situation seem more desperate?

16. In what ways does the poet send distress signals to Aristius Fuscus in lines 63–65?

17. Based on the details of the interchange between the two men in lines 60–72, describe the relationship between the narrator and Aristius Fuscus.

18. The satire draws to a speedy conclusion in lines 74–78. How does Horace's use of words contribute to this sense of rapidity?

19. What would the narrator and the Boor have seen during the course of their stroll down the Via Sacra? What kind of events would have been taking place along the way, and what other sorts of people might be found?

Why Horace?

A Collection of Interpretations
by William S. Anderson

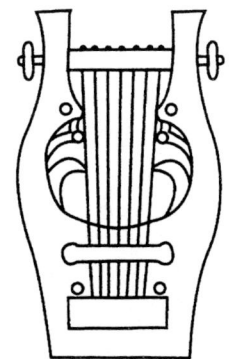

Table of Contents

Introduction

Horace: Odes I
Arthur J. Pomeroy, A Man at a Spring: Horace, *Odes* 1.1
D. W. Thomson Vessey, Pyrrha's Grotto and the Farewell to Love: A Study of Horace *Odes* 1.5
Niall Rudd, Patterns in Horatian Lyric
William S. Anderson, Horace's Different Recommenders of *Carpe Diem* in C. 1.4, 7, 9, 11
Charles Segal, Felices ter et amplius: Horace, *Odes*, *I*. 13
Gregson Davis, *Carmina/Iambi*: The Literary-Generic Dimension of Horace's *Integer Vitae* (C. 1, 22)
Ronnie Ancona, The Subterfuge of Reason: Horace, *Odes* 1.23 and the Construction of Male Desire
H. Akbar Khan, Horace's Ode to Virgil on the Death of Quintilius: 1.24
William S. Anderson, The Secret of Lydia's Aging: Horace, *Odes* 1.25
W. R. Johnson, A Queen, a Great Queen? Cleopatra and the Politics of Misrepresentation
William Fitzgerald, Horace, Pleasure and the Text

Horace: Odes II
A. J. Woodman, Horace, *Odes*, II, 3
John L. Moles, Politics, Philosophy, and Friendship in Horace: *Odes* 2,7
Christopher J. Reagan, Horace, *Carmen* 2.10: The Use of Oxymoron as a Thematic Statement
William S. Anderson, The Occasion of Horace's *Carm.* 2.14

Horace: Odes III
Charles Witke, Horace and the Roman Odes
Michael C. J. Putnam, Horace *Odes* 3.9: The Dialectics of Desire
William Fitzgerald, Horace, Pleasure and the Text (Part 2)
Tony Woodman, *EXEGI MONVMENTVM*: Horace, *Odes* 3.30

Horace: Odes IV
E. A. Fredricksmeyer, Horace, *Odes* 4.7: "The Most Beautiful Poem in Ancient Literature"?

Horace: Satire I.9
William S. Anderson, Horace, The Unwilling Warrior: *Satire* I.9

Bibliography on Horace

xvi + 264 pp. (1999), *Paperback:* ISBN 0-86516-417-7
xvi + 264 pp. (1999), *Hardbound:* ISBN 0-86516-434-7

BOLCHAZY-CARDUCCI Publishers, Inc. ✦ http://www.bolchazy.com

ORAL PROFICIENCY: MUSIC

Carmina Burana
Judith Sebesta

Carl Orff's selections of twenty-four "*cantiones profanae*" from the Middle Ages are explored in this illustrated, dual-language edition featuring the original Latin poems with facing translations and vocabulary, complete vocabulary, bibliography, and study materials. Also included is a literary translation by Jeffrey M. Duban. In addition to medieval woodcuts, this new edition contains seventeen original illustrations by Thom Kapheim.

ISBN 0-86516-268-9

Latin Music Through the Ages
Cynthia Kaldis

Cassette features choral performance of seventeen Latin songs.

ISBN 0-86516-249-2

Book with lyrics, English translations, vocabulary; composer biographies, background on social/historical significance of each song, and illustrations.

ISBN 0-86516-242-5

Latine Cantemus: Cantica Popularia Latine Reddita
translated and illustrated
by Franz Schlosser

This illustrated edition features sixty new Latin translations of popular songs, including nursery rhymes, chanties, folk songs, spirituals, and Christmas carols. Also included are three appendices of traditional Latin favorites, Christmas songs, and well-known Gregorian chants.

ISBN 0-86516-315-4

Schola Cantans
Composed by Jan Novák
Sung by Voces Latinae

A cassette with musical arrangement of **Catullus** (34) *Dianae Sumus in Fide;* **Catullus** (5) *Vivamus Mea Lesbia;* **Catullus** (61) *Collis O Heliconii;* **Horace** (Carm. 1, 22) *Integer Vitae;* **Horace** (Carm. 1,2) *Iam Satis Terris;* **Horace** (epod. 15) *Nox Erat;* **(Anonym.)** *Gaudeamus Igitur;* **Anth. Lat.** (388) *Nautarum Carmen;* **Caesar** (BG 1, 1–3) *Gallia Est Omnis Divisa;* **Carmina Burana** (142) *Tempus Adest Floridum;* **Carmina Burana** (85) *Veris Dulcis in Tempore;* **Martial** (10, 62) *Ludi Magister;* **Phaedrus** (1,13) *Vulpis et Corvus.*

Cassette is accompanied by a libretto with original Latin text and English translation on facing pages. Music score also available.

Cassette
19 pp. (1998), ISBN 0-86516-357-X

Music Score
46 pp. (1998), ISBN 0-86516-358-8

Cassette and Music Score Set
(1998), ISBN 0-86516-404-5

Vergil's *Dido & Mimus Magicus*
Composed by Jan Novák
Conducted by Rafael Kubelik
Performed by the Symphony Orchestra of the *Bayerischer Rundfunk* (Germany)
Original record published by *audite Schallplatten,* Germany

Limited Edition CD (1997)
40-page libretto in Latin, English, and German
ISBN 0-86516-346-4

BOLCHAZY-CARDUCCI Publishers, Inc. ♦ http://www.bolchazy.com

REFERENCES & RESOURCES

Gildersleeve's Latin Grammar
B. L. Gildersleeve and G. Lodge

The classic Latin grammar favored by many students and teachers with two new addtions
- Foreword
  Ward W. Briggs, Jr.
- Comprehensive bibliography
  William E. Wycislo

The 45-page bibliography that accompanies our new reprint is designed primarily but not exclusively for an American audience, comprising scholarship produced on Latin grammar in English during this century.

613 pp. (1895, Third ed.,
Reprint with additions 1997)
Paperback, ISBN 0-86516-353-7

A New Latin Syntax
E. C. Woodcock

xxiv + 267 pp. (1959, Reprint 1987)
Paperback, ISBN 0-86516-126-7

New Latin Grammar
Charles E. Bennett

A model of clear precision, the book uses specific examples from primary sources to help students learn the inflections, syntax, sounds, accents, particles, and word formations of Latin. It also includes a history of the Indo-European family of languages, the stages of the development of the Latin language, and sections on prosody, the Roman calendar, Roman names and definitions, and examples of figures of syntax and rhetoric.

xvi + 287 pp. (1908, Reprint 1995)
Paperback, ISBN 0-86516-261-1

Graphic Latin Grammar
James P. Humphreys

An invaluable quick reference — no need for busy students to keep flipping to the back of the book to look up forms, or search chapters for a review of syntax. These card contain paradigms of regular, irregular, and deponent verbs, nouns, adjectives, pronouns, and numerals; plus charts of prepositions and adverbs; and a guide to syntax of cases and syntax of nouns — all in an easily readable and highly durable format.

(1961, Reprint 1995)
Four 3-hole-punched reference cards, Laminated,
ISBN 0-86516-111-1

New Latin Composition
Charles E. Bennett

ix + 292 pp. (1912, Reprint 1996)
Paperback, ISBN 0-86516-345-6

Latin Prose Composition and Key to Latin Prose Composition
M. A. North and A. E. Hillard

Latin Prose Composition is aimed at helping students to enhance their command of Latin grammar and vocabulary. The exercises have been structured in a manner that gradually enables students to build their Latin prose skills. *Key to Latin Prose Composition* is an invaluable teacher's manual.

Latin Prose Composition
xix + 300 pp. (Reprint 1995)
Paperback, ISBN 0-86516-308-1

Key to Latin Prose Composition
108 pp. (Reprint 1995)
Paperback, ISBN 0-86516-307-3

BOLCHAZY-CARDUCCI Publishers, Inc. ◆ http://www.bolchazy.com

Horace: Selected Odes and Satire I.9
Ronnie Ancona

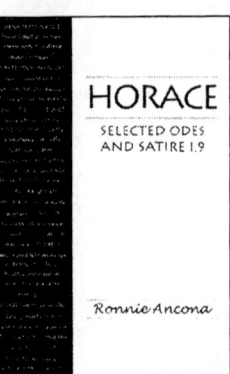

Teacher's Guide
- Latin text in large reproducible format
- Literal translation
- Sample tests
- Extensive, up-to-date bibliography

(1999) Paperback, ISBN 0-86516-430-4

Student Text
- **Introduction** on Horace and his times (including discussion of some of the features of Horace's style that make his work both challenging and exciting to read)
- **Latin text** of all the Horace selections for the 1999 AP Latin curriculum
- **Line-by-line notes**, same page and facing
  - vocabulary • grammatical notes • background notes
- **Complete vocabulary**
- Description of all the **meters** used in the poems
- **Figures of speech** defined, with examples from the Horace poems
- Extensive **bibliography**, including the latest in scholarship on Horace

(1999) Paperback, ISBN 0-86516-416-9

Horace in His Odes
J. A. Harrison

I particularly liked the notes and vocabulary...and the examples given for each meter.
—**Paula Jones**
St. Steven & St. Agnes School

Harrison has divided thirty-three odes into five thematic categories: religion, philosophy, and the brevity of life; friends; love; the countryside; and the Roman state. Also included are: Latin text, introduction, explanatory notes, and vocabulary.

viii + 113 pp. (1981, Reprint 1988) Paperback, ISBN 0-86516-062-7

Selections from Catullus and Horace
Read by Robert P. Sonkowsky
in the *Restored Classical Pronunciation*

At last we have something we can put, with all reasonable confidence, into hands of the student who wants to know what Roman literature sounded like.
—**Gareth Morgan**
Classical World

Booklet and two cassettes (1984) Order # S23800

BOLCHAZY-CARDUCCI Publishers, Inc. ♦ http://www.bolchazy.com

LATIN, HORACE

Horace Satire 1.9: The Boor

For College and Advanced Placement Preparation

edited by
Margaret A. Brucia
Madeleine M. Henry

Reproducible Latin Text
in Large Print
Literal Translation
Study Questions

For Horace of Satire 1.9, it was just one of those days: a pleasant stroll along the Via Sacra becomes a comic struggle when a boorish near-stranger accosts him and can't be shaken. We've all been there—and this is the source of the appeal of Satire 1.9, perhaps the best loved and most familiar of all of Horace's satires.

Bolchazy-Carducci Publishers, Inc.
1000 Brown St., Wauconda, IL 60084
847/526-4344; Fax: 847/526-2867
latin@bolchazy.com; http://www.bolchazy.com

ISBN 086516429-0

9 780865 164291

Horace Satire 1.9

Teacher's Guide

THE BOOR

Margaret A. Brucia
Madeleine M. Henry